Panels & Patchwork

Celebrate a Cozy Christmas

Featuring the Camp Christmas© fabric collection by Janet Wecker–Frisch

LANDAUER BOOKS

Panels & Patchwork™
Celebrate a Cozy Christmas

This book was designed, produced, and published by Landauer Books
A division of Landauer Corporation
3100 NW 101st Street, Urbandale, IA 50322
800-557-2144   www.landauercorp.com

President/Publisher: Jeramy Lanigan Landauer
Director of Operations: Kitty Jacobson
Editor in Chief: Becky Johnston
Managing Editor: Jeri Simon
Art Director: Laurel Albright
Project Designer: Janet Wecker-Frisch
Technical Writer: Rhonda Matus
Editorial Assistant: Debby Burgraff
Photographer: Craig Anderson Photography
We also wish to thank Debbie Brown, Joan Ford, and Diane Tomlinson for their project creations and sewing.

This book printed on acid-free paper.
Printed in USA

10-9-8-7-6-5-4-3-2-1

ISBN 10: 1-890621-56-0
ISBN 13: 978-1-890621-56-8

Introduction

You'll discover the joy of holiday decorating with the ten fast and easy projects shown in this book. Create a cozy cabin Christmas with wool ornaments, buffalo-check place mats, a snuggly quilt and decor inspired by Janet Wecker-Frisch's fabulous Santa images. With these quick-to-create projects you'll still have time for entertaining and making gifts for the friends and family on your list after filling your own home with the warmth of the season.

Begin by purchasing a simple pre-printed panel design that's ideal for use "as is." (Quilt shops and fabric stores offer a wide variety of panel styles and colors.) Refer to the *Basics* section on pages 8–19 for ideas on how to embellish and finish it fast! Start by adding borders to a solo pre-printed fabric panel. Then go beyond basic to combine panels with patchwork, panel motifs with patchwork, and panel fabric coordinates with patchwork. You'll find projects that are quick and easy—pillows, a tree skirt, a Santa wallhanging and an angelic table runner.

Whether you're already comfortable working with fabric and have "made friends" with your sewing machine, or you're new to sewing and quilting, experience the joy that comes from using pre-printed panels to quickly create warm and seasonal decorations for your home.

About the Artist

Inspired by her father, talented artist, Janet Wecker-Frisch has been drawing and painting since childhood. She translated her irresistible watercolor illustrations into her own line of ceramic ornaments. Their success led to licenses for wallpaper and border décor, and fabrics. Janet's *Hungry Animal Alphabet*© characters are the inspiration for a best-selling fabric collection created for South Sea Imports®. New collections from Janet Wecker-Frisch, with more on the drawing board, include *Good Ship Noah*©, *Camp Christmas*©, *Patches & Rhymes*© Mother Goose storybook characters, *Snowfolk Tea Party*©, *Circus Menagerie*© and *Noah's Ark*©.

Janet paints in a studio in her home which she shares with her husband, David. Located in House Springs, Missouri, a suburb of St. Louis, their home is often frequented by visits from their grown children—David, Jacqueline, Katie—and grandchildren—Kaylan, Sydney and John.

Camp Christmas© Fabric Collection

Good Ship Noah© Fabric Collection

Circus Menagerie© Fabric Collection

Patches & Rhymes© Fabric Collection

Snowfolk Tea Party© Fabric Collection

Hungry Animal© Fabric Collection

Contents

Introduction 3

About the Artist ...4

Basics 8

Celebrate with Santa
Santa Wallhanging 20

Santa Tree Skirt 23

Appliqué Ornaments 26

Warm-up to Winter
Two Block Patchwork Quilt .. 28

Bear Paw Pillow 33

A Piece of Heaven

Angel Table Runner 36

Cozy Kitchen

Panel Place Mats 41

Stocking Place Settings ... 42

Snoozin' with Santa

Double Ruffle Santa Pillow ... 45

Box Pillow 47

Basics

◆◆◆◆◆

Learning how to mix pre-printed panels with patchwork will give you more options for many hours of quilting fun—whether you're new to quilting or simply need a refresher. Start by getting acquainted with the many styles of pre-printed panels and their fabric coordinates. Discover how easy it is to make simple patchwork blocks and combine them with pre-printed panel motifs and fabric coordinates. In no time you'll have a beautiful top ready to quilt.

What is a Pre-printed Panel?

A pre-printed panel (also known as "cheater cloth") is a large piece of fabric with a stamped design often featuring a familiar theme such as the Camp Christmas and Good Ship Noah panels shown on these two pages. Frequently the center motif sets the scene for the "story" or theme which is carried out to the fabric edge and repeated in coordinating fabrics with prints, stripes, dots, checks, plaids, and all-over "tosses." Accompanying borders ranging from simple to elaborate complete the collection. To make the best use of a panel, be sure to purchase any and all available coordinates for more design possibilities.

What is a Holiday-themed Pre-printed Panel?

Mixing pre-printed panels with patchwork for festive quilts or wallhangings is a real time-saver during the hectic holiday season. Santa themes, such as the Camp Christmas shown above, are immensely popular because they can be stitched up quickly to use in your own holiday decorating or as gifts. Look for charming fabric coordinates that can be used for smaller seasonal accessories like table runners and coasters. The coordinating snowflakes, pine needles and buffalo check fabrics, as well as the rustic camp "accessory" fabric combine in projects that can be used throughout the winter season.

What is a Flannel Pre-printed Panel?

Recent improvements in heat-stamping designs onto fabric have made it possible to get excellent detail even on such "fuzzy" fabric as flannel or fleece.

Since flannel's softness is most often associated with infants or toddlers, the pre-printed panel designs are themed accordingly. Traditional pink and baby blue are still in vogue, but bright pastels and even blue and red are quite popular. For baby shower or charity quilt gifts, soft green or yellow are a mainstay. Most often the pre-printed panel in flannel is the size of a standard receiving blanket, like the alphabet panel from the Hungry Animal© flannel collection, above.

What are Pre-printed Panel Possibilities?

New quiltmakers find panels ideal for practicing basic quiltmaking techniques. Experienced quiltmakers may already have discovered that pairing pre-printed panels with patchwork is perfect for kids' rooms collections, personalized birthday and holiday gifts or a fast-finish charity quilt.

When considering the purchase of a pre-printed panel fabric collection, look closely at the overall design. A successful pre-printed panel design should incorporate a wide array of characters or stand-alone "motifs" which can be cut out of the panel to mix with patchwork to give the appearance of appliqué.

What Is Patchwork?

Patchwork is any design made of odd pieces of cloth sewn together. Also known as piecing, small cuts of fabric are combined to form blocks that subsequently make up a quilt top.

The quilt top, batting and a backing are layered to form a "sandwich" that is held together by quilting or tying, and then finished with binding along the edges.

Historically, because used clothing was often the only available fabric from which to piece together a bed covering, a creative quiltmaker patched fabrics together to form particular patterns with more visual interest.

Today, an abundant variety of fabrics and techniques offers the quiltmaker endless opportunities for creative sewing expression.

Pre-printed panels are one of many products available today that make it easy to construct a quilt and other decorative accessories.

Many of the projects in this book utilize easily-pieced classic quilt block patterns.

Bear Paw   Goose Tracks

Bear Paw – It's easy to see how this block got its name, with each quadrant in the block resembling the paw of a bear. Half-square triangles and squares make this an easy block to create.

Goose Tracks – This block combines squares and triangle units in each quadrant. Our Goose Tracks block was inspired by the book "Around the Block with Judy Hopkins."

Mixing Pre-Printed Panels with Patchwork

To get you started, here are some ideas for creatively combining pre-printed panels and patchwork (pieced) blocks. Use your imagination to develop your own unique designs.

1. Make pieced blocks from small fabric panels. Border each block with complementary fabric strips to create sashing. Or add sashing with small fabric squares at each corner, creating cornerstones.

2. From a small panel cut out one motif from the design. Appliqué this shape to a background fabric or block.

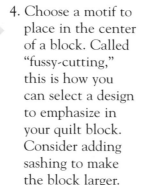

3. Cut out a large motif or several small motifs and appliqué to a complementary background fabric.

4. Choose a motif to place in the center of a block. Called "fussy-cutting," this is how you can select a design to emphasize in your quilt block. Consider adding sashing to make the block larger.

Rotary Cutting

Rotary cutting is a quick-cutting method for making fabric pieces. Special rotary cutting tools have been designed to make cutting fabric easy and accurate.

For successful quick-cutting, always use a specially designed ruler, mat and rotary cutter. These items make cutting easier:

1. 6-1/2" x 6-1/2" rotary cutting ruler

2. 6-1/2" x 18" (or 6" x 18") rotary cutting ruler

3. Rotary cutter (45 mm or 60 mm)

4. Cutting mat (at least 24" in length or width)

Caution: Rotary blades are extremely sharp. If your rotary cutter does not automatically retract, protect yourself from an accidental cut by habitually sliding the blade protector into place each time you set aside the cutter.

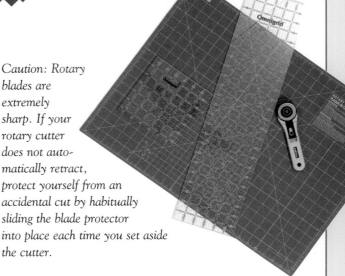

Straightening and Cutting Fabric

Hold the fabric upright to shake out the folds, adjust the edges, and align the selvages. Fold the fabric through the crosswise grain to make the selvages meet, and lay it on your cutting mat. Smooth the fabric, keeping the selvages aligned. Notice that the cut edges—the raw edges—of your fabric may not be aligned.

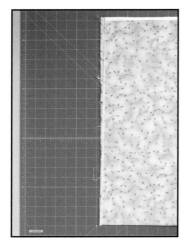

Straightening Fabric

To straighten the fabric edge, use a 6-1/2" square small ruler as a guide to place a 6-1/2" x 24"-long ruler straight on the crosswise fabric grain.

1. Lay the small ruler along the folded edge, placing one of the marked lines on the fold, and the left side of the small ruler near the fabric raw edge.

2. Place the long ruler beside, and to the left, of the small ruler, butting them together smoothly. The right edge of the long ruler should lay against the left edge of the small ruler.

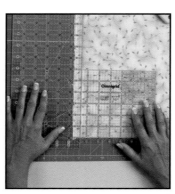

Cutting Fabric

3. When the rulers are aligned with the fabric fold, pull away the small ruler, keeping your left hand on the long ruler to hold it in position. The long ruler should be positioned so its right edge is inside the raw edge of the fabric. Make sure both layers of the folded fabric will be cut when the small ruler is pulled away.

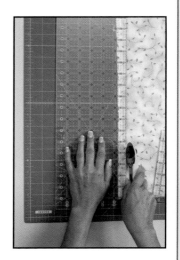

4. Hold the rotary cutter in a vertical position, and with steady pressure roll it along the right edge of the long ruler, from the bottom to the top. As the cutter rolls, walk your fingertips across the surface of the long ruler, maintaining pressure that holds the ruler in place while the rotary blade pushes against it.

When the rotary cutter reaches the top, the raw edge of the cross-grain has been cut and straightened.

After the fabric edge has been straightened, you're ready to begin cutting strips and pieces according to the project you've chosen to make.

Layering and Basting a Quilt

When you have finished your quilt top, it's time to make it into a quilt. A quilt sandwich is made by layering the completed quilt top, quilt batting and quilt backing. The layers are held together with safety pins, called pin basting, until the tying or quilting is completed.

Loft

The loft (thickness) and density of the batting are factors that determine whether you will tie or machine quilt the quilt's layers together. As a general rule, choose less than 1/2" loft polyester batting if you prefer a puffier look that's best for tying together with regularly-placed knots. Choose a low loft—no more than 1/4" thick—batting if you prefer a flatter appearance. Consider that low-loft cotton batting will move better beneath your sewing machine presser foot than a thicker loft batting. If you're uncertain about which batting to purchase, ask a shop clerk for a recommendation.

Layering the Quilt Sandwich

To layer the quilt sandwich you'll need:

1. A hard surface work area, preferably at least as large as the quilt backing.

Note: The tips of safety pins can scratch the work surface, so choose a hard surface that's scratch-resistant. Or, protect the work surface with a rotary mat.

2. A pressed quilt top with all seams laying flat.

3. Batting that measures 4" larger than the quilt top.

4. A pressed backing that measures 4" larger than the quilt top.

5. A roll of masking tape.

6. Safety pins (1" to 1-1/2" in size).

Be sure the backing fabric has been well-pressed. Then, with the wrong side up, lay it on the surface. Smooth the fabric from the center outward.

To hold the backing securely to the surface, place masking tape on one edge toward the middle. On the opposite side, do the same, being sure not to pull the fabric too tightly.

Complete taping on these two sides. Repeat the process on the remaining two sides, taping every six inches.

Lay the batting on top of the quilt backing, carefully smoothing it from the center outward.

Lay the quilt top on the batting. Be sure that the quilt top and the batting are within the edges of the quilt backing. Check and re-check this before beginning to baste.

Pin-Basting the Quilt Sandwich

Safety pins are a quick way to baste a quilt and will hold a quilt sandwich together until the quilt is machine quilted or tied. Safety pins are best for basting when you expect to accomplish quilting in a short period of time.

Plan to baste with thread when you expect to hand quilt—a quilting process that takes more time to accomplish. For thread basting, use a sharp needle and thread, and large running stitches made in a spoke wheel or regular grid pattern. An advantage of thread basting is that thread may be left in a quilt for a longer period of time, whereas safety pins, when left in a quilt sandwich may leave permanent marks or stains.

Basting With Safety Pins

Open and scatter safety pins across the quilt top. With your dominant hand, insert a safety pin into the quilt top, through all layers of the quilt sandwich. Use both hands to close the safety pin. Pins can also be closed with a Kwik Clip™ or other tool such as a grapefruit spoon, held in your non-dominant hand. Insert safety pins randomly, every four to five inches apart across the quilt top to secure the backing.

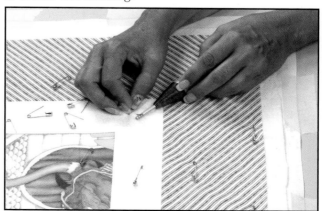

Quilting by Machine

Machine quilting is a quick and attractive way to quilt. If you've safety pin basted your quilt sandwich, be sure to remove the pins as you approach the area you want to quilt. Don't attempt to sew over the safety pins.

Two machine quilting options are available if you choose to quilt it yourself. You can either sew all straight-line stitches using a walking foot. Or, you can free-motion stitch, sewing curves, circles and other random shapes using only your hands to guide the fabric. For free-motion quilting you'll need a quilting foot.

Sewing Machine Set-up for Quilting

Set up your sewing machine for quilting. If you plan to straight-line machine quilt, attach a walking foot. If you don't have a walking foot, use your machine's straight-stitch foot. For free-motion quilting, attach a darning foot. You'll also need to lower the feed dogs (refer to your sewing machine owner's manual), or cover them so you can move the quilt sandwich smoothly beneath the needle.

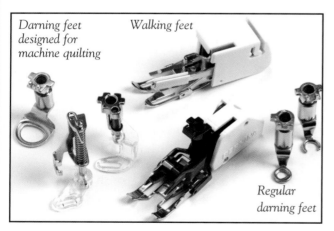

Darning feet designed for machine quilting

Walking feet

Regular darning feet

Needle for Machine Quilting

Change your sewing machine needle to a quilting needle or a jean's needle, size 80 or 90. This needle has a larger shaft that will more readily puncture the three layers of the quilt sandwich.

Thread for Machine Quilting

Choose nylon monofilament thread for machine quilting if you want to sew nearly invisible quilting stitches. Thread your sewing machine with the monofilament thread on top and for the bobbin choose a thread color that closely matches the quilt backing. Or, choose the same color of thread for the top and the bobbin. It's helpful to test your stitches before beginning to quilt. Make sure your sewing machine tension is adjusted for your thread (refer to your sewing machine owner's manual).

Design Options for Machine Quilting— Straight-Line or Free-Motion

Simple, straight-line machine quilting, also called utility quilting, is easy to accomplish and will hold the quilt layers together. Whenever possible, begin quilting from the center outward to prevent wrinkles from being quilted into the quilt top or back. Choose from one of these straight stitching options:

1. *Stitch-in-the-ditch quilting.* This quilting requires no marking. Simply stitch along the seam lines as closely as possible.

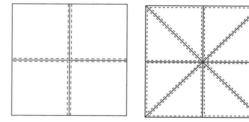

2. *Grid quilting.* Sew a simple grid at regularly spaced intervals on the quilt surface. Align a long rotary ruler with the intersections of blocks. Lightly draw quilting lines with chalk, marking pencil, or a wash-out pen. Quilt on the lines.

Free-motion quilting is a bit more challenging, but definitely fun. Lower the feed dogs and use a quilting foot for:

3. *Stipple quilting.* (This is also known as meander quilting.) No marking is needed to create these random curves that flow across a quilt surface.

For greater visual interest, try a combination of several quilting designs including straight-line, stitch-in-the-ditch and free-motion quilting.

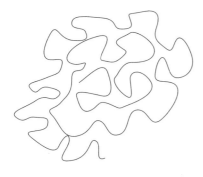

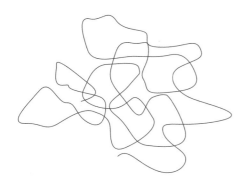

Binding a Quilt

The last step in finishing your quilt is to add the binding. Binding is a fabric strip that encases the outside edges of the quilt. Double-fold binding is most commonly made because it's durable. As the name implies, the quilt edge is wrapped with two layers of fabric. A 2-1/4" to 2-1/2"-wide fabric strip, is folded and sewn to the front of the quilt along the edge, then folded and hand sewn to the quilt back.

If your quilt will hang on the wall, add a sleeve to the top edge of the quilt back at the same time the binding is sewn.

Piecing Binding

If you've cut the binding strips according to the pattern instructions, you'll need to sew strips together to obtain the length needed. Here's how:

1. Position a binding strip, right side up, horizontally in front of you.

2. To the left and at a perpendicular angle to the horizontal strip, position another binding strip right side down on top of the horizontal strip.

3. From corner to corner, across the overlapping areas, draw a diagonal line.

4. Sew on the drawn line.

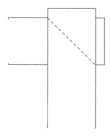

5. Trim away the excess fabric to measure a 1/4" seam allowance.

6. Press open the sewn seam to reduce bulk.

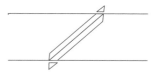

7. Fold wrong sides together and press.

Sewing the Binding to the Quilt Top

Align the raw edges of the binding strip to the raw edge of the quilt top. Sew the binding to the quilt top, using a 1/4" seam allowance.

Trimming the Quilt Sandwich

After machine sewing the binding to the quilt sandwich, cut away excess fabric and batting. Exercise caution! Be sure to cut away only the excess—not the folded binding or the binding corners.

Place the quilt on the rotary cutter mat with the binding on top. Use the long rotary ruler to measure 3/8" outward from the binding stitching line. Rotary cut along the ruler to remove all but 3/8" of the backing and batting.

Overview of Continuous Binding with Mitered Corners

This binding is applied in one long, continuous fabric strip. By folding the binding at each corner, extra fabric is allowed to hand-sew a miter into the corner.

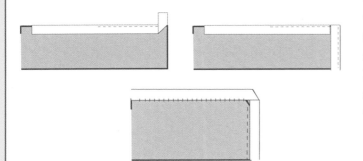

Hand Sewing the Binding to the Quilt Back

After trimming away any excess material on the quilt edge, hand sew the binding in place. Lay the quilt on your lap with the backing facing up. Fold and secure, using metal hair clips, the binding to the back of the quilt.

Knot one end of a needle with thread that matches the color of the quilt backing. Begin hand sewing at any point, securing the binding fold over the machine stitches. Stitch from right to left using a slip stitch.

Take care at each corner to fold and tuck fabric into a diagonal seam, hand sewing it into place. When the binding and four corners have been sewn down on the quilt back, turn the quilt over and hand sew the front side of each mitered corner seam.

If you've added a sleeve to your quilt, also hand sew the folded edge of the sleeve to the quilt back, making sure to take stitches that will not show on the quilt front.

Adding a Hanging Sleeve to a Quilt

To display a quilt on a wall, the best time to add a sleeve or rod pocket to the quilt is at the same time that binding is sewn to the quilt.

The instructions that follow are for creating a sleeve that holds a hidden rod. When the quilt is hung on the wall, nothing is visible except the quilt.

Depending on the size of the quilt you're hanging, you'll need to determine what width of flat lath or molding, or the diameter of the dowel rod you'll need that will reliably support the quilt's weight. A 1" to 2"-wide board gives good support and keeps a quilt flat against the wall. For small quilts, try using a wooden yardstick as a sleeve rod.

Measure, Cut, and Add a Sleeve

1. Decide which way you want to hang the quilt and measure across the top.

2. Deduct 2" from this number to obtain the finished length of the sleeve.

3. Add 3" to the finished length to obtain the unfinished length. This measurement allows a 1-1/2" fold at each sleeve end.

4. Measure the width of the lath, molding or dowel used to hang the quilt. Multiply the width by 2, add 1" for ease of insertion and 1/2" for seam allowances to determine the unfinished width of the sleeve.

5. Using the unfinished measurements, cut out a sleeve from the same fabric as the quilt backing.

6. At each end of the sleeve make a 1-1/2" fold to the wrong side; press.

7. Fold the sleeve length in half, wrong sides together; press.

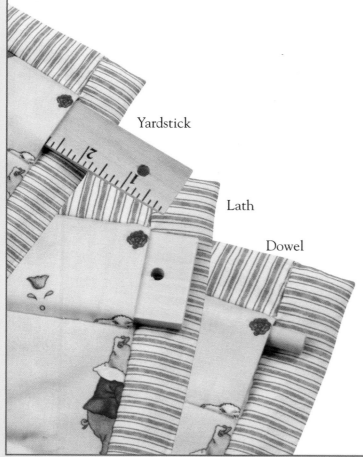

Yardstick

Lath

Dowel

8. Align the raw edges of the sleeve with the top raw edge of the quilt back. Be sure the sleeve is positioned on the back of the quilt; pin.

9. Align the raw edges of the binding to the top raw edges of the quilt front; pin.

10. Attach the binding and sleeve to the quilt top with a 1/4" seam allowance.

11. Using a slip stitch, hand-sew the folded edge of the sleeve to the quilt back. Avoid taking stitches that will show on the quilt front. Finish by sewing the binding to the back of the quilt.

Measure, Cut, Drill and Hang a Board

1. Deduct 1" from the measurement of the quilt top and cut a 1" to 2-1/2"-wide, flat board that length.

2. Approximately 1/3" to 1/2" from each end of the board, drill a hole that will accommodate a nail head.

3. Position the board on the wall and mark the location of the drilled holes.

4. Hammer nails through the marks.

5. Insert the drilled board through the sleeve.

6. Hang the quilt.

Measure, Cut and Hang a Dowel Rod

1. Deduct 1" from the measurement of the quilt top and cut a dowel that length.

2. Position the dowel to place marks on the wall 1/4" to 1/3" in from each end of the dowel.

3. Hammer nails through these marks.

4. Insert the dowel rod through the sleeve.

5. Hang the dowel on the nails, making sure the quilt edges cover the nail heads.

Santa Wallhanging

Add holiday color and charm to a wall or above a mantel with a Santa wallhanging created from a pre-printed panel. It allows you to decorate quickly and with style.

Materials

Finished size: 36-1/2x48-1/2"

1 pre-printed character panel

1-1/2 yards of green print fabric for backing

5/8 yard of black-and-white check fabric for outer border

1/2 yard of red print fabric for inner border and binding

40x52" rectangle of quilt batting

Cut the Fabric

From pre-printed character panel, cut:
  1— 28-1/2x40-1/2" center rectangle

From green print, cut:
  1—40x52" backing rectangle

From black-and-white check, cut:
  4—4-1/2x44" strips; from the strips cut 2—4-1/2x40-1/2" side outer borders and 2—4-1/2x36-1/2" top and bottom outer borders

From red print, cut:
  4—1x44" inner border strips; from the strips cut 2—1x40-1/2" side inner borders and 2—1x28-1/2" top and bottom inner borders
  5—2-1/4x44" binding strips

Sew with right sides together using 1/4" seam allowances unless otherwise specified.

Instructions

Assemble the Quilt Top

1. Fold the inner border strips in half lengthwise with wrong sides together; press. Place the 40-1/2" red print side inner border strips on the right and left edges of the center rectangle, aligning the raw edges of the inner border with the long raw edges of the center rectangle. Sew in place.

2. Sew the 28-1/2" red print top and bottom inner border strips to the top and bottom edges of the center rectangle as in Step 1.

3. Sew the 40-1/2" black-and-white check side outer borders to the left and right edges of the center rectangle as shown in Diagram A. Press the seam allowances toward the outer borders.

Diagram A

4. Sew the 36-1/2" black-and-white check top and bottom outer borders to the top and bottom edges of the quilt as shown in Diagram B. Press the seam allowances toward the outer borders.

Diagram B

Complete the Quilt

1. Smooth out the backing on a flat surface with the wrong side up and center the batting on the backing. Center the quilt top, right side up, on top of the batting. Baste the layers together.

2. Beginning in the center and working outward, machine quilt through all layers as desired. Our quilt was machine quilted along the design lines of the pre-printed quilt panel and outer border and in the ditch along the inner edge of the outer border.

3. Sew the short ends of the 2-1/4"-wide binding strips together with diagonal seams to form one long binding strip. Trim the excess fabric, leaving 1/4" seam allowances. Press the seam allowances open. Fold the strip in half lengthwise with wrong sides together; press.

4. Beginning at the center of one edge of the quilt, place the binding strip on the right side of the quilt top, aligning the raw edges of the binding with the raw edges of the quilt top. Fold over the beginning of the binding strip about 1/2". Sew through all layers 1/4" from the raw edges, mitering the corners (refer top age 18). Trim away the excess binding, leaving 1/2" at the end to overlap the beginning of the strip. Trim the batting and backing even with the quilt top.

5. Fold the binding to the back of the quilt to cover the machine stitching; press. Slip stitch the folded edge of the binding in place or sew in the ditch along the binding, catching the folded edge of binding on the back of the quilt.

Santa Tree Skirt

Snowflakes and Santas alternate panels on this octagonal tree skirt. Surrounded by red and black-and-white check, it's perfect for the den or that hide-away cabin in the woods.

Materials

Finished size: 54" diameter

Graph paper (optional)

4 yards of black-and-white check fabric for outer border, backing and binding

1-1/4 yards of black snowflake print fabric for triangles

1-1/4 yards of Santa print fabric for triangles

1/4 yard of red print fabric for inner border

Straight edge and pencil

60x60" piece of quilt batting

Enlarge the skirt triangle pattern on page 25 200% onto graph paper or use a photocopy machine. Add 1/4" seam allowances beyond the drawn lines and cut out the completed pattern. Sew with right sides together using 1/4" seam allowances unless otherwise specified.

Cut the Fabric

From black-and-white check, cut:
> 2—30x60" backing rectangles
> 8—4-1/4x25" outer border strips
> 2-1/4"-wide bias strips to total 275" of binding

From black snowflake print, cut:
> 4 skirt triangles

From Santa print, cut:
> 4 skirt triangles

From red print, cut:
> 4—1-1/2x44" strips; from the strips cut 8—1-1/2x20" inner border strips

Instructions

Assemble the Tree Skirt Top

1. Center and sew a 1-1/2x20" red print inner border strip to the bottom edge of each skirt triangle. Press the seam allowances toward the triangle.

2. Center and sew a 4-1/4x25" black-and-white check outer border strip to the inner border on each triangle. Press the seam allowances toward the outer border.

3. Use a straight edge and a pencil to draw lines on the inner and outer borders to follow the side edges of each skirt triangle as shown in Diagram A. Trim the borders on the drawn lines.

Diagram A

4. Referring to the Tree Skirt Assembly Diagram, sew the long edges of the triangles together in a circle, alternating the snowflake and Santa prints and leaving one seam unstitched for the center back opening. Press all seam allowances in the same direction.

Complete the Tree Skirt

1. Sew together the long edges of the 30x60" black-and-white check backing rectangles. Press the seam allowances to one side.

2. Smooth out the backing on a flat surface with the wrong side up and center the batting on the backing. Center the skirt top, right side up, on top of the batting. Baste the layers together.

3. Beginning in the center and working outward, machine quilt through all layers as desired. Our tree

skirt is machine quilted in the ditch along all seam lines of the skirt triangles and borders. In addition, the snowflake triangles and outer border are filled with freehand quilting and the Santa triangles are filled with a 3" square grid.

4. Sew the short ends of the 2-1/4"-wide binding strips together with diagonal seams to form one long binding strip. Trim the excess fabric, leaving 1/4" seam allowances. Press the seam allowances open. Fold the strip in half lengthwise with wrong sides together; press.

5. Beginning at the middle of one center edge of the tree skirt, place the binding strip on the right side of the front of the tree skirt, aligning the raw edges of the binding with the raw edges of the tree skirt front. Fold over the beginning of the binding strip about 1/2". Sew through all layers 1/4" from the raw edges, mitering the corners (refer to page 18). Trim away the excess binding, leaving 1/2" at the end to overlap the beginning of the strip. Trim the batting and backing even with the tree skirt front.

6. Fold the binding to the back of the tree skirt to cover the machine stitching; press. Slip stitch the folded edge of the binding in place or sew in the ditch along the binding, catching the folded edge of the binding on the back of the tree skirt.

Tree Skirt Assembly Diagram

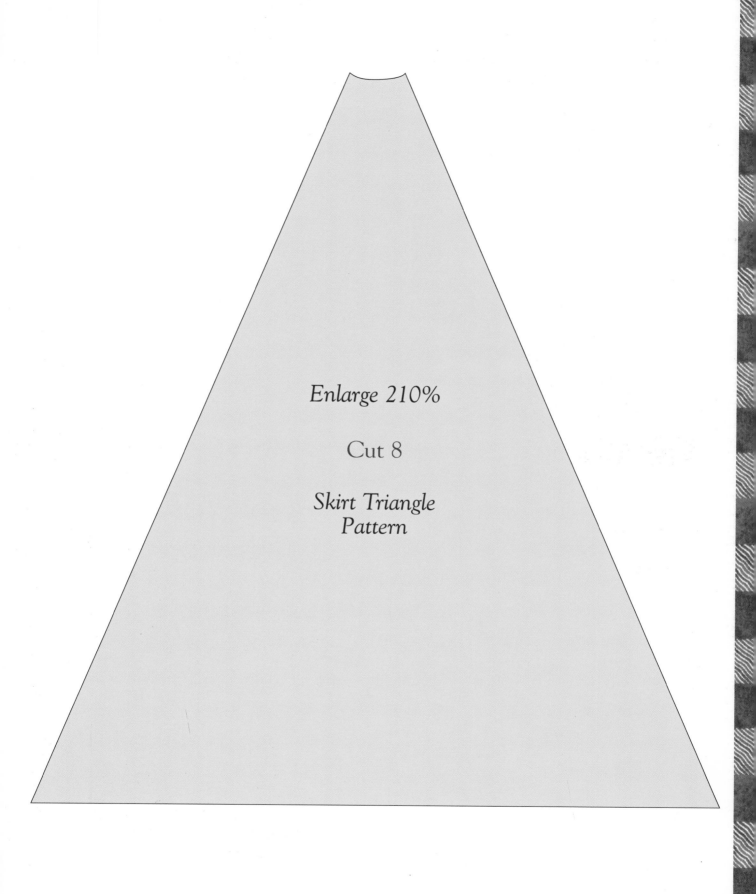

Enlarge 210%

Cut 8

Skirt Triangle Pattern

Appliqué Ornaments

Decorate a holiday tree or create a string of garland with these fast-to-finish wool felt appliqué ornaments. Fussy-cut figures from fabric and hand or machine appliqué to wool felt stars and trees.

Materials

Finished size: 4" to 6" tall

Paper-backed fusible webbing

Scraps of holiday-motif fabric

Coordinating wool felt

Pinking shears

Sulky® Rayon or Poly Deco Decorative Thread

#3 pearl cotton

Large-eyed needle

Instructions

1. Use a pencil to trace one of the patterns provided or draw your own shape onto the paper side of the fusible webbing. Cut out the fusible web shape about 1/4" beyond the drawn line.

2. Fuse webbing shape to the wrong side of the holiday-motif fabric, centering the motif in the shape. Carefully cut out the shape and remove the paper backing.

3. Position the fabric appliqué shape on coordinating wool felt and fuse in place. Use a pinking shears to cut the felt about 1/2" to 3/4" beyond the edges of the appliqué shape.

4. Machine buttonhole stitch over the edges of the appliqué shape using decorative thread in color of your choice.

5. Sew a pearl cotton hanging loop to the center top of the ornament.

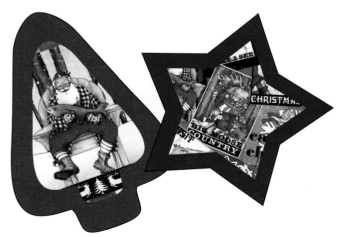

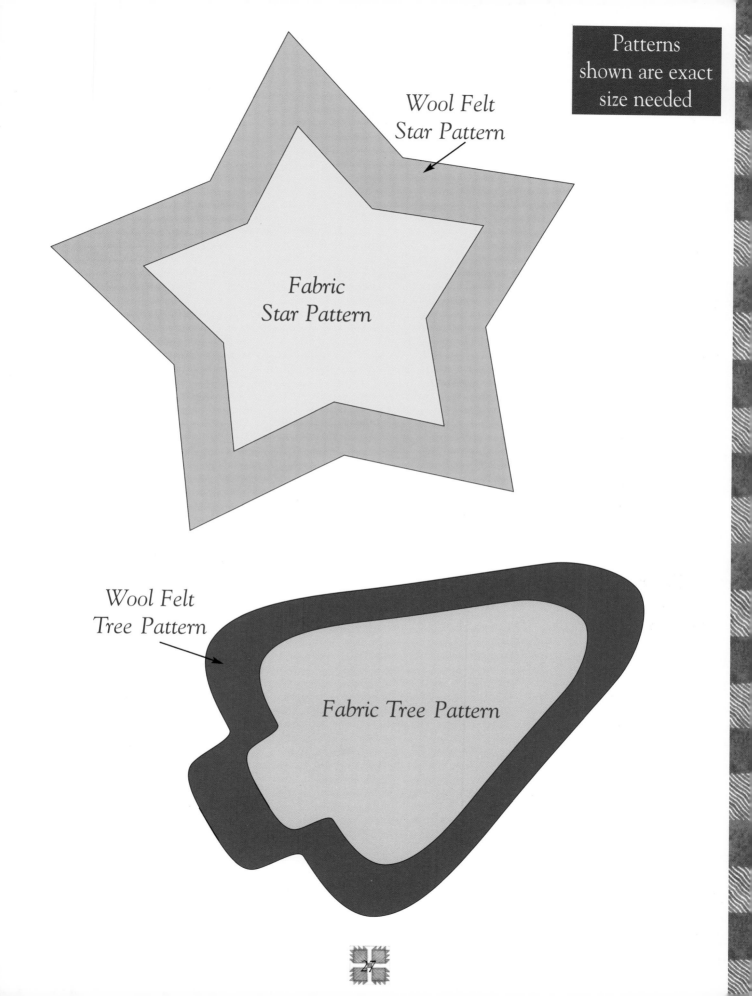

Wool Felt
Star Pattern

Fabric
Star Pattern

Wool Felt
Tree Pattern

Fabric Tree Pattern

Two Block Patchwork Quilt

Escape winter's chill with this warm and inviting quilt that's big enough for two. You'll be tempted to stay snuggled-up all season long

Materials

Finished size: 77-1/2x77-1/2"

5-3/4 yards of green-and-white check fabric for backing and binding

3-3/4 yards of Santa stripe border fabric for middle border

2 yards of green print fabric for blocks

1-3/4 yards of green snowflake fabric for outer border

1-5/8 yards of cream snowflake fabric for blocks

82x82" rectangle of quilt batting

Cut the Fabric

From green-and-white check, cut:
    2—41-1/2x82" backing rectangles
    6"-wide bias strips to total 325" of binding

From Santa stripe border, cut:
    4—5x65" middle border strips; cut so the green-and-white check border is at the top edge and the black tree and deer border is at the bottom edge of the strips

From green print, cut:
    4—6-1/2x44" strips; from the strips cut 20—6-1/2" squares
    5—2-7/8x44" strips; from the strips cut 60—2-7/8" squares
    4—2-1/2x44" strips; from the strips cut 16—2-1/2x8-1/2" strips and 5—2-1/2" squares
    2—4-1/2x44" strips; from the strips cut 16—4-1/2" squares
    1—5-1/4x44" strip; from the strips cut 8—5-1/4" squares

From green snowflake print, cut:
    8—7-1/2x44" outer border strips

From cream snowflake print, cut:
    2—8-7/8x44" strips; from the strips cut 8—8-7/8" squares
    6—2-1/2x44" strips; from the strips cut 20—2-1/2x8-1/2" strips and 24—2-1/2" squares
    5—2-7/8x44" strips; from the strips cut 60—2-7/8" squares
    1—5-1/4x44" strip; from the strip cut 8—5-1/4" squares

Sew with right sides together using 1/4" seam allowances unless otherwise specified.

Instructions

Assemble the Bear Paw Blocks

1. With right sides together, layer the 2-7/8" squares in pairs, using a green print with each cream snowflake print. Cut the layered squares in half diagonally as shown in Diagram A to make 120 pairs of triangles.

Diagram A

2. Sew 1/4" from the diagonal edge of each pair as shown in Diagram B to make half-square triangles. Press open with the seam allowances toward the green fabric.

Diagram B

3. Sew together 3 half-square triangles and 1—2-1/2" cream snowflake print square as shown in Diagram C. Press the seam allowances away from the green print fabric. Repeat to make 20 square/half-square triangle units.

Diagram C

4. Sew together 3 half-square triangles as shown in Diagram D. Press the seam allowances toward the green print fabric. Repeat to make 20 half-square triangle units.

Diagram D

5. Arrange a 6-1/2" green print square and one of each pieced unit from Steps 3 and 4 as shown in Diagram E. Sew the half-square triangle unit to the 6-1/2" square; press seam allowances toward the square. To complete a bear paw, attach a square/half-square triangle unit and press seam allowances toward the square. Repeat to make 20 bear paws.

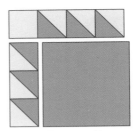

Diagram E

6. Arrange the bear paws from Step 5, 4—2-1/2x8-1/2" cream snowflake strips, and a 2-1/2" green print square as shown in Diagram F. Sew the pieces together in rows and then sew the rows together to complete one Bear Paw block. Repeat to make five Bear Paw blocks.

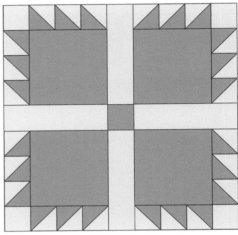

Diagram F

Assemble the Goose Tracks Blocks

1. With right sides together, layer the 5-1/4" squares in pairs, using a green print with each cream snowflake print. Cut the layered squares in quarters diagonally as shown in Diagram G to make 32 pairs of triangles.

Diagram G

2. Sew 1/4" from a straight edge of each pair to make 16 of each two-triangle unit as shown in Diagram H. Press the seam allowances toward the green fabric.

Diagram H

3. Sew together a 4-1/2" green print square and 2 pieced units from Step 2 as shown in Diagram I. Press the seam allowances away from the green square. Repeat to make 16 square/triangle units.

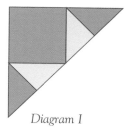

Diagram I

4. Cut the 8-7/8" cream snowflake print square in half diagonally to make 16 triangles. Sew a large cream snowflake print triangle to one of each pieced square/triangle units from Step 3 as shown in Diagram J to make 16 lilies. Press the seam allowances toward the large cream snowflake print triangle.

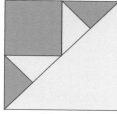

Diagram J

5. Arrange the lilies from Step 4, 4—2-1/2x8-1/2" green strips and a 2-1/2" cream snowflake print square as shown in Diagram K. Sew the pieces together in rows and then sew the rows together to complete one Goose Tracks block. Repeat to make four Goose Tracks blocks.

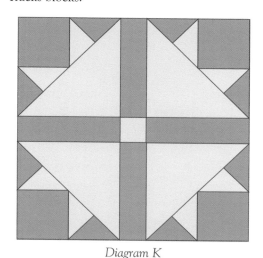

Diagram K

Assemble the Quilt Center

1. Lay out the Bear Paw and Goose Tracks blocks on a flat surface in 3 rows of 3 blocks, referring to the Quilt Assembly Diagram on page 32 to alternate the blocks in a checkerboard fashion.

2. Sew the blocks together in rows. Press the seam allowances of each row to one side, alternating the direction with each row.

3. Sew the rows together to complete the quilt center. Press the seam allowances toward the center row.

Assemble the Quilt Top

1. To miter the inner border, center and pin a 5x65" inner border strip to one edge of the quilt center. Sew together, beginning and ending the seam 1/4" from the edges of the quilt center as shown in Diagram L. Press the seam allowances toward the border.

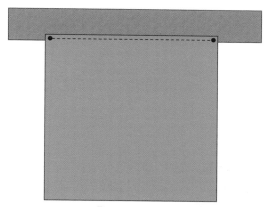

Diagram L

2. Sew a 5x65" inner border strip to each remaining edge of the quilt center as in Step 1.

3. Working with one corner at a time, draw a diagonal line on the wrong side of the top strip from the corner of the stitching to the point where the two strips meet at the raw edges as shown in Diagram M. Reposition the strips so the bottom border is on top and draw a second line in the same manner.

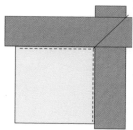

Diagram M

4. With right sides together, match the drawn lines and pin as shown in Diagram N. Beginning at the inside corner, sew the border strips together directly on the drawn lines. Trim the excess fabric, leaving a 1/4" seam allowance. Press the seam allowances in one direction. Repeat Steps 3 and 4 to miter each corner.

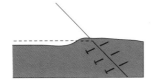

Diagram N

5. Seam the 7-1/2"-wide green snowflake print outer border strips as needed to make four 80" lengths. Follow Steps 1 to 4 to attach the outer border and miter the corners.

Complete the Quilt

1. Sew together the long edges of the 41-1/2x82" green-and-white check backing rectangles with a 1/2" seam allowance. Press the seam allowances to one side.

2. Smooth out the backing on a flat surface with the wrong side up and center the batting on the back. Center the quilt top, right side up, on top of the batting. Baste the layers together.

3. Beginning in the center and working outward, machine quilt through all layers of the quilt. Outline quilt each piece of the Lily blocks and the square and strip pieces of the Bear Paw blocks. Quilt diagonal lines 1" apart in the large cream snowflake print triangles and large green print squares. Quilt in the ditch along the edges of each border. In addition, quilt along the design lines of the middle border and freehand quilt to fill the outer border.

4. Sew the short ends of the 6"-wide binding strips together with diagonal seams to form one long binding strip. Trim the excess fabric, leaving 1/4" seam allowances. Press the seam allowances open. Fold the strip in half lengthwise with wrong sides together; press.

5. Beginning at the center of one edge of the quilt, place the binding strip on the right side of the quilt top, aligning the raw edges of the binding with the raw edges of the quilt top. Fold over the beginning of the binding strip about 1/2". Sew through all layers 1" from the raw edges, mitering the corners (refer to page 18). Trim away the excess binding, leaving 1/2" at the end to overlap the beginning of the strip. Trim the batting and backing even with the quilt top.

6. Fold the binding to the back of the quilt to cover the machine stitching; press. Slip stitch the folded edge of the binding in place or sew in the ditch along the binding, catching the folded edge of the binding on the back of the quilt.

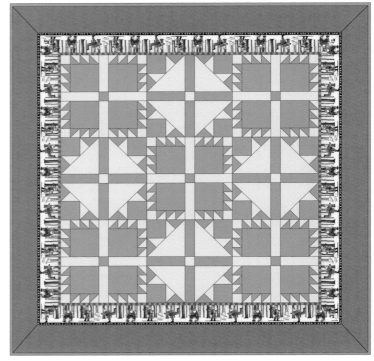

Quilt Assembly Diagram

Bear Paw Pillow

Waiting for ol' Saint Nick to arrive is a bit easier when relaxing on a Bear Paw pillow bordered with Santa enjoying a winter wonderland.

Materials

Finished size: 23-1/2x23-1/2"

1-1/2 yards of Santa stripe border fabric for border

1-1/2 yards of green snowflake print fabric for backing

3/8 yard of black snowflake print fabric for binding

1/4 yard of green print fabric for block

1/4 yard of cream print fabric for block

25" square each of muslin and quilt batting

13" length of 3/4"-wide sew-on hook-and-loop fastener

14x14" pillow form

Cut the Fabric

From Santa stripe border, cut:
    4—5-1/4x24" borders

From green snowflake print, cut:
    2—23-1/2x27" backing rectangles

From black snowflake print, cut:
    3—3x44" binding strips

From green print, cut:
    1—2-3/8x44" strip; from the strip cut 12—2-3/8" squares
    4—5" squares
    1—2" center square

From cream print, cut:
    1—2-3/8x44" strip; from the strip cut 12—2-3/8" squares
    1—2x44" strip; from the strip cut 4—2x6-1/2" strips
    and four 2" squares

Instructions

Assemble the Block

1. With right sides together, layer the 2-3/8" squares in pairs, using a green print with each cream print. Cut the layered squares in half diagonally as shown in Diagram A to make 24 pairs of triangles.

Diagram A

33

2. Sew 1/4" from the diagonal edge of each pair as shown in Diagram B to make half-square triangles. Press open with the seam allowances toward the green fabric.

Diagram B

3. Sew together 3 half-square triangles and 1—2" cream print square as shown in Diagram C. Press the seam allowances away from the green print fabric. Repeat to make four square/half-square triangle units.

Diagram C

4. Sew together 3 half-square triangles as shown in Diagram D. Press the seam allowances toward the green print fabric. Repeat to make four half-square triangle units.

Diagram D

5. Arrange a 5" green print square and one of each pieced unit from Steps 3 and 4 as shown in Diagram E. Sew the half-square triangle unit to the 5" square; press seam allowances toward the square. To complete one Bear Paw, attach a square/half-square triangle unit and press seam allowances toward the square. Repeat to make four Bear Paws.

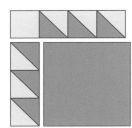

Diagram E

6. Arrange the Bear Paws from Step 5, 4—2x6-1/2" cream print strips and a 2" green print center square as shown in Diagram F. Sew the pieces together in rows and then sew the rows together to complete one Bear Paw block.

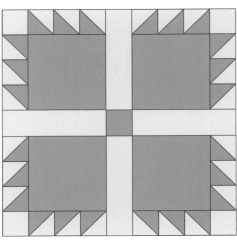

Diagram F

Complete the Pillow Front

1. To miter the border, center and pin a 5-1/4x24" strip to one edge of the block. Sew together, beginning and ending the seam 1/4" from the edge of the block as shown in Diagram G. Press the seam allowances toward the border.

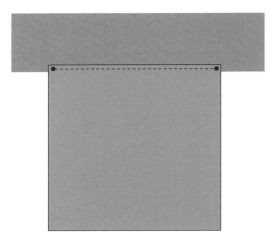

Diagram G

2. Sew a 5-1/4x24" border strip to each remaining edge of the block as in Step 1.

3. Working with one corner at a time, draw a diagonal line on the wrong side of the top strip from the corner of the stitching to the point where the two strips meet at the raw edges as shown in Diagram H. Reposition the strips so the bottom border is on top and draw a second line in the same manner.

Diagram H

4. With right sides together, match the drawn lines and pin as shown in Diagram I. Beginning at the inside corner, sew the border strips together directly on the drawn lines. Trim the excess fabric, leaving a 1/4" seam allowance. Press the seam allowances in one direction. Repeat Steps 3 and 4 to miter each corner.

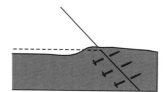

Diagram I

5. Smooth out the muslin square on a flat surface and center the batting on the muslin. Center the pillow front, right side up, on top of the batting. Baste the layers together.

6. Machine quilt in the ditch along all sewn edges of the 2x6-1/2" cream print strips. Trim the batting and muslin even with the raw edges of the pillow front.

Complete the Pillow

1. Fold each backing rectangle in half with wrong sides together, aligning the 23-1/2" edges opposite the fold. Press and baste along the raw edges of each backing rectangle.

2. Smooth the pillow front, right side down, on a flat surface. Position a back rectangle on one half of the pillow front, aligning three edges with the folded edge near the center. Position the second backing rectangle over the remaining half of the pillow front in the same manner. Pin, then sew the overlapped areas on the back together around the edges; do not sew to the front at this time.

3. Sew the hook side of the fastener to the wrong side of the upper backing piece, centering it along the folded edge. Mark the location for the loop side of the fastener on the right side of the lower backing piece and sew the fastener in place.

4. Edge-stitch along the fold of the upper backing piece from each end of the fastener to the raw edge as shown in Diagram J.

Diagram J

5. Reposition the back on the front with wrong sides facing and pin together. Sew through all layers, quilting in the ditch along the inner edge of the border, creating a flange.

6. Sew the short ends of the 3"-wide black snowflake print binding strips together with diagonal seams to form one long binding strip. Trim the seam allowances to 1/4" and press open. Fold the strip in half lengthwise with wrong sides together; press.

7. Beginning at the center of one edge of the pillow cover, place the binding strip on the right side of the pillow front, aligning the raw edges of the binding with the raw edges of the pillow cover. Fold over the beginning of the binding strip about 1/2". Sew through all layers 1/2" from the raw edges, mitering the corners. Trim away the excess binding, leaving 1/2" at the end to overlap the beginning of the strip.

8. Fold the binding to the back of the pillow to cover the machine stitching; press. Slip stitch the folded edge of the binding in place or sew in the ditch along the binding, catching the folded edge of the binding on the back of the pillow.

9. Insert the pillow form in the cover through the hook and loop fastener opening.

Angel Table Runner

*Guests will consider you a heavenly host when
they spot this beautifully quilted table runner.
It will add a special touch to a holiday buffet or side table.*

Materials

Finished size: 17-1/2x49-1/2"

1-1/4 yards of black snowflake
print fabric for backing and
inner border

3/4 yard of red print fabric for
outer border and binding

3/8 yard of Christmas-motif
print fabric for center rectangle

20x52" rectangle
of quilt batting

Cut the Fabric

From black snowflake print, cut:
    2—20x26-1/2" backing rectangles
    3—1-1/2x44" strips;
    from the strips cut 2—1-1/2x11" side inner borders
    and 2—1-1/2x43" top and bottom inner borders

From red print, cut:
    4—3-1/2x44" outer border strips
    4—2-1/4x44" binding strips

From Christmas-motif print, cut:
    1—9-1/2x41-1/2" center rectangle

*Sew with right sides together
using 1/4" seam allowances
unless otherwise specified.*

Instructions

Assemble the Table Runner Front

1. To miter the inner border, center and pin a 1-1/2x43" black snowflake inner border strip to the long edges of the 9-1/2x41-1/2" center rectangle. Sew together, beginning and ending the seam 1/4" from the short edges of the center rectangle as shown in Diagram A. Press the seam allowances toward the border.

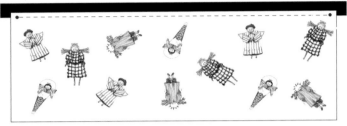

Diagram A

2. Sew the 1-1/2x11" black snowflake inner border strips to the short edges of the center rectangle as in Step 1.

3. Working with one corner at a time, draw a diagonal line on the wrong side of the top strip from the corner of the stitching to the point where the two strips meet at the raw edges as shown in Diagram B. Reposition the strips so the bottom border is on top and draw a second line in the same manner.

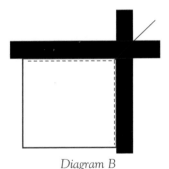

Diagram B

4. With right sides together, match the drawn lines and pin as shown in Diagram C. Beginning at the inside corner, sew the border strips together directly on the drawn lines. Trim the excess fabric, leaving a 1/4" seam allowance. Press the seam allowances one direction. Repeat Steps 3 and 4 to miter each corner.

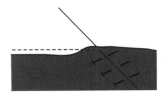

Diagram C

5. Seam the 3-1/2"-wide red print outer border strips as needed to make two 20" lengths and two 52" lengths. Follow Steps 1 to 4 to attach the outer border and miter the corners, sewing the 20" lengths to the side edges and the 52" lengths to the top and bottom edges.

Complete the Table Runner

1. Sew together the 20" edges of the 20x26-1/2" backing rectangles with a 1/2" seam allowance. Press the seam allowances to one side.

2. Smooth out the backing on a flat surface with the wrong side up and center the batting on the backing. Center the table runner front, right side up, on top of the batting. Baste the layers together.

3. Beginning in the center and working outward, machine quilt through all layers as desired. Our table runner was machine quilted along the design lines of the Christmas-motif center rectangle and in the ditch along both edges of the inner border. Machine quilt 1/4" and 1" from the inner edge of the outer border. In addition, the background areas of the center rectangle are filled with freehand quilting.

4. Sew the short ends of the 2-1/4"-wide binding strips together with diagonal seams to form one long binding strip. Trim the excess fabric, leaving 1/4" seam allowances. Press the seam allowances open. Fold the strip in half lengthwise with wrong sides together; press.

5. Beginning at the center of one edge of the table runner, place the binding strip on the right side of the front, aligning the raw edges of the binding with the raw edges of the table runner front. Fold over the beginning of the binding strip about 1/2". Sew through all layers 1/4" from the raw edges, mitering

the corners (refer to page 18). Trim away the excess binding, leaving 1/2" at the end to overlap the beginning of the strip. Trim the batting and backing even with the table runner front.

6. Fold the binding to the back of the table runner to cover the machine stitching; press. Slip stitch the folded edge of the binding in place or sew in the ditch along the binding, catching the folded edge of the binding on the back of the table runner.

Meander quilting, also referred to as stippling, gives a wonderful, textured look to the table runner below. This type of quilting, as its name suggests, needs no pattern since it winds randomly through the area you are quilting. For a smoother, more professional look try to avoid overlapping your stitching lines. The angels in our table runner were outline-stitched before the background was quilted.

Panel Place Mats

*Give family and friends a warm holiday welcome with
Santa-inspired place mats. Perfect for dining at
your Christmas table or in front of a crackling fireplace.*

Materials

Finished size: 20x13"

Materials listed will make two place mats.

1/2-yard of red snowflake print
fabric for backing

1/4-yard of Santa-motif print
fabric for center front

1/3-yard black-and-white check
fabric for border

1/4-yard small-print fabric
for binding

22x15" rectangle of
quilt batting

Cut the Fabric

*Cutting and instructions are for one place mat. Repeat steps to
make second place mat.*

From red snowflake print, cut: 1—22x15" rectangle for backing

From Santa-motif print, cut: 1—15-1/2x8-1/2" rectangle
for center front

From black-and-white check, cut:
2—2-3/4x44" strips; from the strips cut 2—2-3/4x22" top
and bottom borders and 2—2-3/4x15" side borders

From small-print, cut:
2—2-1/4x44" binding strips

*Sew with right sides together using 1/4" seam allowances unless
otherwise specified.*

Instructions

Assemble the Place Mat Front

1. To miter the border, center and pin a 2-3/4x22" black-and-
    white check border strip to the top and bottom edges of the
    15-1/2x8-1/2" Santa-motif center rectangle. Sew together,
    beginning and ending the seam 1/4" from the side edges of
    the center rectangle as shown in Diagram A. Press the seam
    allowances toward the border.

Diagram A

41

2. Sew the 2-3/4x15" black-and-white check border strips to the left and right edges of the center rectangle as in Step 1.

3. To miter corners refer to instructions for assembling the table runner front, steps 3—5 on page 38.

Complete the Place Mat

1. Smooth out the backing rectangle on a flat surface with the wrong side up and center the batting on the backing. Center the place mat front, right side up, on top of the batting. Baste the layers together.

2. Machine quilt through all layers along the design lines of the Santa-motif and black-and-white check fabrics.

3. Sew the short ends of the 2-1/4"-wide binding strips together with diagonal seams to form one long binding strip. Trim the excess fabric, leaving 1/4" seam allowances. Press the seam allowances open. Fold the strip in half lengthwise with wrong sides together; press.

4. Beginning at the center of one edge of the placemat, place the binding strip on the right side of the front, aligning the raw edges of the binding strip with the raw edges of the place mat front. Fold over the beginning of the binding strip about 1/2". Sew through all layers 1/4" from the raw edges, mitering the corners. Trim away the excess binding, leaving 1/2" at the end to overlap the beginning of the strip. Trim the batting and backing even with the place mat front.

5. Fold the binding to the back of the placemat to cover the machine stitching; press. Slip stitch the folded edge of the binding in place or sew in the ditch along the binding, catching the folded edge of the binding on the back of the place mat.

Stocking Place Settings

Fill stockings with napkins and silverware for unique and festive holiday place settings guests are sure to admire.

Materials

Finished size: 12" tall

1/2 yard of red snowflake print fabric for stocking front, back and lining

8-3/4x4-3/4" rectangle of border print fabric for cuff

15" square of lightweight quilt batting

Sulky® Polyester Invisible Thread

Enlarge the stocking pattern 150% with a photocopy machine; cut out the pattern. Sew with right sides together using a 1/2" seam allowance unless otherwise specified.

Cut the Fabric

From red snowflake print, cut:

    1—15" square for quilting

    2 stocking linings, reversing one of the shapes

Instructions

1. Smooth the batting on a flat surface. Center the 15" square of red snowflake print fabric, right side up, on the batting; pin the layers together. Thread your sewing machine with invisible thread and machine quilt the layers together in a 1-1/2" diagonal grid as shown in Diagram A.

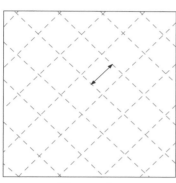

Diagram A

2. Use the stocking pattern to cut a stocking front and back from the quilted fabric, reversing one of the shapes.

3. Sew the quilted stocking front to the back, leaving the top edges open. Trim the seam allowances and clip the curves. Turn the stocking right side out.

4. Sew the stocking lining pieces together, leaving the top edge open. Trim the seam allowances and clip the curves; do not turn.

5. Slip the lining inside the stocking with wrong sides together. Baste the top edges together.

6. Sew together the short edges of the cuff, forming a circle. Press the seam allowances open and turn right side out. Press under 1/4" at the bottom edge for hem; sew in place.

7. Slip the cuff inside the stocking with the right side of the cuff facing the lining. Align the raw edges, centering a Santa-motif on the front of the stocking. Sew the cuff to the stocking, easing the cuff to fit. Fold the cuff down over the right side of the stocking.

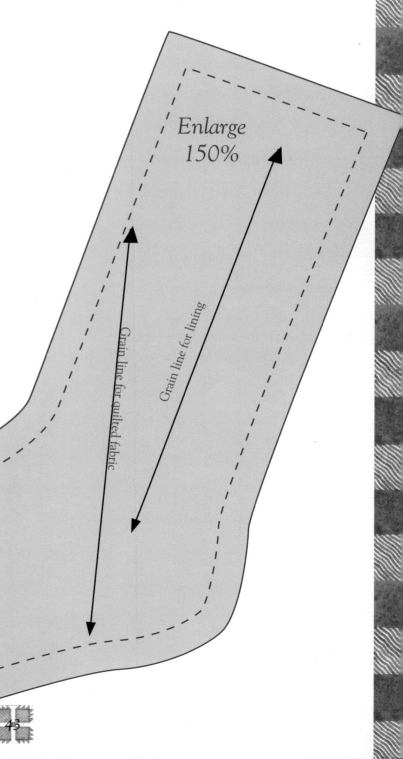

Enlarge 150%

Grain line for quilted fabric

Grain line for lining

Double Ruffle Santa Pillow

Accent your favorite room with a pillow highlighted by framed Santas and Christmas tree cut-outs. The feeling of the season is completed by a double ruffle of snowflakes.

Materials

Finished size: 39-1/4x18-1/2", including ruffle

Pre-printed framed Santa print fabric for front

7/8 yard of red snowflake print fabric for back and ruffle

3/4 yard of black snowflake print fabric for ruffle

1/4 yard of cream snowflake print for sashing and border

Polyester fiberfill

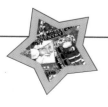

Cut the Fabric

From pre-printed framed Santa print, cut:
    3—7-1/4x9" front Santa rectangles
    2—3x7" front tree rectangles

From red snowflake print, cut:
    3—5x44" ruffle strips
    1—12-1/2x33-1/4" back rectangle

From black snowflake print, cut:
    3—8x44" ruffle strips

From cream snowflake print, cut:
    2—1-1/2x44" strips;
    from the strips cut 4—1-1/2x9"
    and 4—1-1/2x3" sashing strips
    2—2-1/4x44" strips;
    from the strips cut
    2—2-1/4x33-1/4"
    and 2—2-1/4x9" border strips

Sew with rights sides together using 1/4" seam allowances unless otherwise specified.

Instructions

Assemble the Pillow Front

1. Sew the 1-1/2x3" cream snowflake print sashing strips to the top and bottom edges of the 3x7" front rectangles as shown in Diagram A. Press the seam allowances toward the rectangles.

2. Sew the 1-1/2x9" cream snowflake print sashing strips to the left and right edges of the 3x7" rectangles as shown in Diagram B. Press the seam allowances toward the rectangles.

3. Sew together the 7-1/4x9" front rectangles and the pieced units from Step 2 as shown in Diagram C. Press the seam allowances away from the sashing.

Diagram A

Diagram B

Diagram C

4. Sew the 2-1/4x9" cream snowflake print border strips to the left and right edges of the pillow front. Press the seam allowances toward the center.

5. Sew the 32-1/4x33-1/4" cream snowflake print border strips to the top and bottom edges of the pillow front. Press the seam allowances toward the border.

Complete the Pillow

1. Sew the 5" edges of the red snowflake print ruffle strips together to form a big circle. Press the seam allowances open. With wrong sides together, fold the strip in half lengthwise and press. Sew gathering threads through both layers 1/2" and 1/4" from the raw edges. Pull on the gathering threads until the circle of ruffle fits around the perimeter of the pillow front as shown in Diagram D, slightly rounding the corners. Adjust the gathers evenly, pushing a little extra into the corners of the pillow. Pin and baste the ruffle to the pillow front.

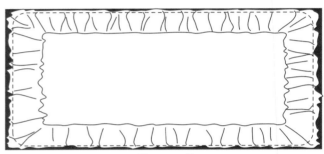

Diagram D

2. Repeat Step 1 with the 8"-wide black snowflake print ruffle strips. Sew it atop the red snowflake print ruffle.

3. Sew the pillow front to the back with a 1/2" seam allowance, leaving a 6" opening in the bottom edge.

4. Trim the seam allowances and turn the pillow cover right side out. Stuff the pillow firmly with polyester fiberfill. Sew the opening closed.

Box Pillow

Santa Claus takes center stage on this box pillow trimmed with seasonal fabric and green piping.

Materials

Finished size: 3x18x18"

1-1/8 yards of Santa print fabric for front border, sides and back

1/2 yard of green print for piping and appliqué

1/3 yard of cream print for center square

1—5x5-5/8" block from framed Santa fabric for appliqué

Paper-backed fusible webbing

9" square of Sulky® Tear-Easy stabilizer

Sulky® KK 2000 temporary spray adhesive

Sulky® Rayon or Poly Deco Decorative Thread in red

4-1/2 yards of narrow cotton cording

3x18x18" box pillow form

Cut the Fabric

From Santa print, cut:
 2—5x44" strips; from the strips cut 4—5x20" borders
 2—4x38" side strips
 1—19" back square

From green print, cut:
 1-1/2"-wide bias strips to total 160" of piping
 1—6" appliqué square

From cream print, cut:
 1—11" center front square

From fusible webbing, cut:
 1—6" square
 1—5x5-5/8" rectangle

*Sew with right sides together using **1/2"** seam allowances unless otherwise specified.*

Instructions

1. To miter the border, center and pin a 5x20" Santa print border strip to one edge of the cream print center front square. Sew together, beginning and ending the seam 1/2" from the edges of the center square as shown in Diagram A. Press the seam allowances toward the border. Repeat with each border strip.

Diagram A

2. Working with one corner at a time, draw a diagonal line on the wrong side of the top strip from the corner of the stitching to the point where the two strips meet at the raw edges as shown in Diagram B. Reposition the strips so the bottom strip is on top and draw a second line in the same manner.

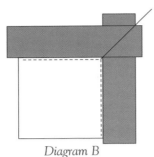

Diagram B

3. With right sides together, match the drawn lines and pin as shown in Diagram C. Beginning at the inside corner, sew the border strips together directly on the drawn lines. Trim the excess fabric, leaving a 1/4" seam allowance. Press the seam allowances one direction. Repeat Steps 2 and 3 to miter each corner.

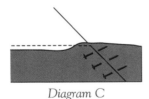

Diagram C

4. Following the manufacturer's instructions fuse a corresponding webbing shape onto the wrong side of the green print and the framed Santa appliqué shapes. Remove the paper backing. Referring to the photograph on page 44, position and fuse the green print appliqué on the pillow front and the framed Santa appliqué on the green appliqué.

5. Center the 9" square of tear-away stabilizer behind the cream print center square on the back of the pillow front with temporary spray adhesive. Satin stitch over the edges of the appliqués with red decorative thread. Tear away the stabilizer from the back of the pillow front.

6. To make piping, sew the short ends of the piping strips together to form one long strip. Press the seam allowances open. Center cording on wrong side of strip and fold fabric over the cording, matching long edges. Use a zipper foot to sew through both fabric layers close to the cording.

7. Beginning at the center bottom of the pillow front, pin piping to the right side of the front, slightly rounding corners with raw edges facing out. Clip seam allowance of piping at corners for a better fit. Overlap ends of piping, trimming off excess piping. Baste piping to pillow front using zipper foot. Repeat for the pillow back.

8. Sew the short ends of the side strips together to form one long strip. Press the seam allowances open and press under 1-1/2" at one end. Pin the side strip to the right side of the pillow front, beginning with the pressed end at the center of the bottom edge; trim the opposite end to overlap the pressed end.

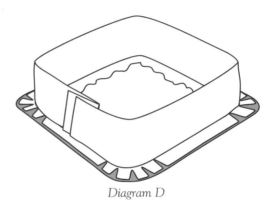

Diagram D

9. Sew the side strip to the pillow front as shown in Diagram D, sewing atop the piping basting stitches and clipping seam allowance of side band as you sew for a better fit. Sew together the overlapped area on the opposite edge of the side band to secure the band's correct length.

10. Sew the opposite edge of the side strip to the pillow back in the same manner, taking care to position the pillow back corners in line with the pillow front corners and leaving a 10" opening in the bottom edge.

11. Turn the pillow cover right side out. Insert the pillow form and sew the opening closed.